Hags on Tractors

∽⃝

Penny Johnson

A Publication of The Poetry Box®

Poems © 2024 Penny Johnson
All rights reserved

Editing & Book Design by Shawn Aveningo Sanders
Cover Design by Shawn Aveningo Sanders
Author Photo provided by Penny Johnson
Photo Editing by Robert R. Sanders

No part of this book may be republished without permission from the author, except in the case of brief quotations embodied in critical essays, epigraphs, reviews and articles, or publisher/author's marketing collateral.

ISBN: 978-1-956285-78-9
Published in the United States of America
Wholesale Distribution by Ingram Group

Published by The Poetry Box, December 2024
Portland, Oregon, United States
website: ThePoetryBox.com

Finish each day and be done with it. You have done what you could. Some blunders and absurdities no doubt crept in: forget them as soon as you can. Tomorrow is a new day. You shall begin it serenely and with too high a spirit to be encumbered with your old nonsense.

—Ralph Waldo Emerson

Enter Macbeth: How now, you secret, black and midnight hags! What is't you do?

—Shakespeare

Contents

Like a Matriarchal Elephant	7
As I walk the plank	12
Never Safe	14
Late Lunch Dakota Café	19
New Brand of Syncopation	20
Upper Peoh Fire-Lookout	24
Below the Dragon's Breath	25
Ripped Along Its Very Own Fault Line	28
Burn Witches	31
As If the Sky Can Be Pressed	34
Acknowledgments	37
Early Praise	39
About the Author	41

Like a Matriarchal Elephant

1.

Look. There is no one here. There is never anyone else here this stream of damp musk, sawdust and beige mushroom. Look. This, metered gauge where now the needle jousts. It skews. My lassitude. My fortitude. And then, a single gasp of hyperventilation.

2.

One morning I bought it. Bought it new. Off the ship. Off the docks. From another land. Coax it home in all its enamel and cobalt blue. Nonnecrotic and scratch resistant. Non-sclerotic and felted in black hydraulic lines. Like an elephant's trunk. The nimble wrap. The twist. Reaching. Reaching. Tractors survive an expanse of time like all the other matriarchs.

3.

Remember to stretch forward from the waist. Palm open. Clasp this new vocabulary with its array of tiger-orange and lapis-lazuli. Knobs. Clickers right. Clickers left. Oh lord, see? It is fanning its giant ears. As if they flap in warning. And this sprig of a tail, its own hygienic three-point-hitch. Gargled growl of its power-take-off.

4.

Watch as I swing wide the maw, the tusks, the teeth barely missing my own roof line. All in practice to tilt this black bucket just so. Back blade just above the crushed gravel. And even now. Look. It carries me. We, working in tandem. We, as the neighbors drive by. One after the other. White pickup with the blue handicap sticker. Gray pearl pickup. Three black pickups in a drawn-out-row. Don't look I say and squint my eyes.

5.

Those neighbors. Those same pickups. They lean out their windows. Lean into the knubs of their elbows on their window frames. They will gawk. They will turn to their passenger and say she doesn't know what she is getting into. She won't make it through the first winter.

6a.

They will laugh

6b.

They have always laughed. But it is my ribs that hurt from all their laughing.

7.

Tonight, I brew this soup of vermillion tomatoes plucked out of frost, whose cracks are barely sealed over with opaque filament. This glue. Stir the pot and dabble in a wide expanse of gray sage, the needle-nose of evergreen rosemary. As the crescent moon rises, I will bury the paper-white garlic, the red fall potatoes deep in earth that lies in the sparkle of its own ice crystals.

8.

Plant for spring.

9.

And don't even think to ask how strong this elephant is. Not with these solid-state cotter-pins. These chromed sway bars. This howdah rides high and slides within an endless luxury of lube. Black and grated, both split brake pedals cup my soles. Oh lord. Look. It spins on a dime. This new realm that shimmies in blue.

As I walk the plank

between broccoli's thick joe-green leaves. This shitake-tinged morning where wild-fire-smoke louvers sun. This grease layered smoke cannot be discounted. Furnace of noon squirms us flat and we would all be overexposed without this opaque layer. Even the tiger-striped red cat crouches beneath this unguent of smoke.

Jack fell over dead at his dining room table after the first fires. Taylor Bridge. His heart unbuckled under the weight of smoke even as the snow started up. Quixotic. I walked into the sour scent of death to sit with his wife. We perked a dark roast coffee. The coroner took a while in coming.

Now, I twist on the sprinklers dark and spotting the green peppermint in a shiver and sluice of well-water. Of aquifer. Of arsenic. As the red cat leaps between mustard greens so steeped in their own juice they would burn my mouth. Not even the goats will touch them.

And look, the blue-veined kale sprouting into its own life, cycles free-faced from dirt. Curling its edges like stripped ribbon. But come fall those ruffles will web solid with sticky aphids. Look at the way the bumble bees syrup their lift off. Rounder than fat thumbed blackberries. Bees bloomered with stiff-stalk legs, in a rich powder of lavender where both flowers and bees are justified to each other within their own armies.

Lavendula: garden escapee and usurper that transfixes this patch. Sprouts up in fennel. Sprouts up between the logs of firewood. Where weeds lock arms under the finite spray of water and morning glory vines tip the towering magenta holly hocks. Stop.

Don't stoop to rub the white belly fur of this red cat. He will nail you. Soon I take the chain saw where the pink petals of wild rose white-knuckle the woven-wire fence. Here we live barely nurtured with a talent to surrender under the ultimatum of a zillion seedheads. And look, this rooting desert-vine whose runners pepper with sticker-claws. Stop.

Stand still a second. Watch the creek tinkling through even as it plays its own hurdy-gurdy. Here, springs up the wild iris.

Here, where horses and the ghosts of more horses pack their hooves in cool mud while their lips purse to pluck the feathered heads off horsetail. Here where the wild scouts of September will snap-crackle through underbrush.

The varnished brown elk, bugle back and forth, back and forth, heralds of rut and begin their royal procession.

Never Safe

Plus all this chili while my pasture gate springs unhinged. And this is my enunciation,

for a knotted gut, to prop this inside corner up, six-inch log of charred firewood

while wind whips sixty mph. Face square into shards of all my past in such tiny flakes.

Oh man, so jagged edged. Stagger to steady unyielding metal rungs, creak on ice, before

my knotted gut, how to prop this corner up, at the very least prop of charred firewood.

Then the entirety jolts loose again. Listen. The key always is the inside corner. Heave,

jagged edged. Stagger to steady unyielding metal rungs. Crack of ice, before it skewers

wavering against exact alignment, top to bottom, against all that solitary and howls.

the entirety jolts loose again. Listen. The key is always this inside corner. Heave.

Incoming night sucking marrow. Inside this bowl of solitary, darkness stirs a syllabub

skewer it in exact alignment, top to bottom, hinged against all that howls solitary

and despair shivers each talus. Rails buck. Uncorks every single knuckled carpal: Pop!

Incoming night sucking marrow. Inside this bowl of solitary. Darkness a syllabub

champagned to the point of pop. Top jolts. Reckless dive. Who do you think whose

despair that shivers each talus. Rails buck. Un-knuckled every single brittle carpal: Pop!

you are, huh? Shouts each past-husband opaque in their march up from the barn

Champagned at the point of pop. Top jolts. A reckless dive.
Who do you think? Damn

Such slick smiles. Who do you think you are asks my father?
My mother: bared.

Who do you think you are demands each past-husband
opaque marching, malingering

teeth in my mother's skull. I could never keep her safe. I
tried. I tried. But stop! Loose and

such slick smiles. Who do you think you are demands my
father? My mother bares

uncountable losses while I carry lead-ropes, both hands as if
the loose limbs of long-gone

teeth in my mother's skull, as if I could ever keep her safe.
Just. Stop. Now. Cut loose

the baby. Listen. We used to know the songs. Remember?
We used to sing the words.

These losses. Carry lead ropes in my own two hands. Carried like loose limbs long-gone

and I am so sorry I say as I clip the maroon to scarlet to black and finally speckled blue-

the baby's gone. We used to know the songs remember? We used to sing the words.

This gate. Wrangle the fucking thing. Beat it into simple submission, past corrosion

and I am so sorry I say as I clip the maroon to scarlet to black and finally speckled blue.

Husbands whip like crabbed brown leaves back inside the barn. My father-mother curd

inside this gate. Wrangle the fucking thing. Beat it into a simple submission of the past-

shrinks like snails inside my pancreas. Tie these lines across all this vacant space. Howl as husbands whip like crabbed dead leaves back inside the barn. My father-mother curd

from a closeted clot of obscenities. It is closed. Now my mare will be safe as wind sucks

back, shrunk like snails inside my pancreas. Crosshair lines across vacant space. Howl

in polished moon. Horizon. This enunciation by clouds steamed in a mole of chili red sauce.

Late Lunch Dakota Café

Redolent of rank meat. Black moon fingernails
crusted mud. This perfume scent of vinegar
rasping an old kennel, a new black-mouth-cur.
This dog so smart he hitched a ride all the way
from Tallahassee. But this afternoon, we slide
together. Cuffs slick, March wet snow, manure.
We are pasted onto nothing, again, again and this
bean barley soup. Curried. You say your husband
smashed the car into the barn or the house. Now
he speaks of you only in third person. Swiss cheesed.
We hold so still in a beaded incantation star struck,
steamed between curled cups of thick-knuckled hands.

New Brand of Syncopation

1.

Nineteen excuses not to walk into the shop of all men wafting diesel with the skin of their eyes puckered and sucked blind behind themselves:

this resolute me

walks in regardless

with a forward tilt

2.

Skewered hot dogs, salt and grease, scrim of burnt coffee, powdered nondairy creamer. And a cashier scanning prices. And now my own diesel treatment rocks on the counter and words pull like stretched toffee between us as he says: You don't want…what do you run?

It's not my car, I stammer.

It's for my tractor, I say with perfect elocution.

3a.

Now, the next plunge into this downhill slope of misconception. But hold on. In this origami moment, where cashier and I both know how carefully our paper is creased and what lines are splayed in this heart-felt-soup of appropriation or let it be skin-to-skin hand grasping.

3b.

This is a simple weeknight's soup of quartered zucchini. Mince of rosemary. Chop of chili into which I promise to launch tiny dumplings so heavy they scud rock-bottom.

4.

So toothsome.

5.

Crisp snow flecks your New Holland Blue. This. You, yourself, a new line of skyline where I live cheap as thick porcelain but you, my tractor, you ride unshackled. Yet still, you fire and die. Fire and die. And staggered with fear, hands empty, once again I am congealing into a thick white, poultry gravy.

6.

Every artery of me now flows with coagulated leftovers

        of my white boned heritage

        of my unconscionable expectations

        of my inscrutable female gendered tenacity

a tenacity beyond belief. Even now I release my breath. Thin lips. Silver whistle. I realign myself, like pig-pink silk within each exhale and during the next inhalations, the black grossgrain ribbon of black holes cycles between us. This is our shared terra firma and our slewed sky of a slivered moon, sprinkled pinprick stars.

7a.

Even this far along in my inner encyclopedia of a single roustabout, palm's lifeline, an eight-legged arachnoid squirms down my cochlea and still I pour more amber diesel-anti-gel and still I double-back with both coral-red hot-water bottles whose faded rubber is now paled from their own viscous hot-cherry beginnings. I press these warm bodies against this jello-tank praying it's your exact receptor on your lumbar spine.

7b.

Mercy is all I have left to whisper.

8.

And grip the very atoms stunned still and hold myself like ice trapped within its fall. One more time, for this new brand of syncopation as I say, please let me not misunderstand you.

And, of course, this cannot be what startles the orange spark. This is not what snaps both our joints to coordinate with your own steady thrumming, not what unpacks the both of us, let loose now, free running within the shavings of our steaming breath.

Upper Peoh Fire-Lookout

Horses' dark manes snarl into wickiup brush while
our own gray-boned-fingers meld and crisscross
pluck at a melanoma snap, breath even, so resilient
a resilience to my own ivory hairs' Hiroshima crown.
Dreadlocked. Your steel-blue, rib-eyed from behind
and this years' green timothy bagged, hangs high-lined
within a soft sift of black pine boughs. Cloud-whipped
frost moon rises even while sighing that nothing is truly
ever all this crisped and pearly white except snowflakes
spattering in a flurry untethered on ice-black horse fur.
Do you even remember pale halfmoons in pink shell fingernails?
Now, our fungus-horn-toes collude with pine needles and earth.

Below the Dragons' Breath

This kind of litigation where faucet spits air. I clench
a stationary toothbrush. Nothing. Sour-mouth, circuit-
breaker and then every frost-free water bib here on down.
Check. Hallowed and buried, cistern empty and unstrung

       upright stationary toothbrush. Sour mouthed, circuitous
       axle of what's habitable, free-wheeling and a nonnegotiable
       in litigation of a deep bellied cistern unstrung and hollowed.
       Behind the stacked shade of the barn, slivered green twine

              axle of a freewheeling into nonnegotiable water litigation
              skimming chestnuts and a thick pariah of horse manure
              behind the flat shadowed barn, a shivered green twine
              like the failed body of a garden snake's unarmored skin

[. . .]

chestnuts on a thick porridge of horse manure
and the red handled bib stands itself sky-high
like a coiled body of a garden snake unarmored.
Skinned. Say grace and then say grace even louder

       and the red bib stands, its handle sky high, sun's
       morning, glowering a heat that corkscrews blind.
       Say grace and then yank the handle down. Crackles
       this circuit box and flicks a vein like a drip, drip, drip

              morning sun skewers heat, now corkscrews blind
              then this poised needle hits the vein. Water pulls
              and circuit box flicks into a vein like a tap tap tap
              beats deep below, drawn off bitter brush and sage

then this poised needle flicks into vein. And water flows
beneath smoke, the fire, burnished burn-backed throat
in deep beating, deep bellows, igniting bitter brush, sage
havoc of dragons-breath as fire somersaults tangerined sky

        below the smoke, this fire, taste thick-blacked, in a dry throat
        now surrender the raspberries, weeds chest high, sweep low
        in havoc of marauder fire-dragons, somersault in a fire-sky
        as I press inside a single sweet memory of a cool tagine

                  quixotic salt
                  harissa olives

          surrender now the raspberries, the weeds
                chest high and
          tongued tang of preserved lemon
          bites against sour-mouthed teeth.

Ripped Along Its Very Own Fault Line

1.

Hoist the three-twine-bale off the haystack. All this dead-weight hooked one-handed. This is the final release. Watch it hula its broad hips. Unmoored now from its loft, moment of flight, to splat on concrete.

2.

Like my first friend named Kathy. How to swivel our pelvis. How to pucker our lips. Link your arms around his neck she says. Rest your head just so. Hula your hips. Relish this plunge. And now, here comes the thump.

3.

The aluminum envelopes. The way he shimmies it out of his jean pocket. Tears it open with his front teeth. Never yet, in all these years, have I watched, my eyes fast on the pine tree branches glowing in the night's own sky. How one-handed, it fits like a glove. Later he will toss it on the forest ground, the mice. The gnawing mice.

4.

Always, these razor-tooth mice
even here, in the dim cavern of this barn where the brightest blue tractor swigs all available space in one breathless draught. Those candy colors. The scarlet, the sky blue. All those two seaters. Canvas tops. Those way-ago, far-gone years. And the way he spread his navy-blue coat over the ground. As if he would keep doing this the rest of my life. No matter what.

5a.

Oh those cars. Us girls. The specifications recited by heart. Do you remember each specification? Of course you do. Etched for all time in black and white. Coiled in our intestines. Digested like vitamins. Like DNA. But I tell you now:

5b.

A tractor will crank-over, never hemorrhage with no malice in its own slick pools of hydraulic fluid widening on concrete. A tractor will not guzzle. It will not careen off at midnight in a mean-mouth tiff. Or forget to come home, the children in bed and snow hanging off the roof. These black tires, so knubby. Go ahead. Throw your arm over the diameter. Slow pucker your lips and whistle inside an endless exhale. Rest your head and look, it will always let you brace your left hip against its expanse.

6.

Between this and then, the dark and yellow porch lights, three giant white dogs. As they curl, they sink into the sour smell of old dog beds along this dry porched precipice. They wait for you. A cloak of snow toplines each vertebra of their backs. And still they wait. Snow shimmies midflight then rises even within its fall. How many times can one woman do the same?

7.

Wait for this sourdough. It will come out of the roasting oven with one end surprisingly flat. Its crust torn. Deeply scarred. Charred underneath. Against all this, cast this single loaf up into the air, rip loose its patch of skin seared to the black pan and fling its belly, white and cracked steaming one more time out into the open.

Burn Witches

Hair silver as mine, woman in a cart drives two blond ponies. Supple leather lines.

Shouting a chorus to my half-feral dog, white and tall as timber wolves while I quick

unclip the black mare's lead within illusion of barbed wire security and a snug gate.

Herself: drives a staccato trot, both yellowed ponies, our voices braid in syncopation

shouting a chorus to my half-feral dog, white and tall as a wolf while I fast unclip

yelling leave-it-quit-it but this dog is long and races outside our voices' validation.

Herself: the punctured trot of two gold ponies in our voices braided syncopation

within this song she stops so I rise a bravado in this, my need to know did you ever shout leave-it-quit-it but this dog is long and races outside our voices' validation

did you ever see yourself this solitary, cracked yolk thrown from its white. Relentless

within this song. She stops while I rise bravado, the need to know how we know

how do we remember? They used to burn witches. As if you and I didn't already

see ourselves this solitary like a cracked yolk thrown from its white. Relentless

what happens to women who brandish uncommon thoughts. Those fires.

They used to burn witches you know. As if our very bones don't already know

those fires, mountains of flames, sanctifications. But it's not easy to burn a body.

What happens to women who brandish uncommon thoughts. Those flames.

And smoke drifts. My own black mare crescendos, flinging alabaster hooves.

Those fires, mountain's sanctification. But our bones know it's not easy to burn

as we scatter all the ways there are to slip off rocks, plunge into corned snow.

And smoke drifts. My own black mare crescendos, flinging alabaster hooves

firecracker a final trumpet blast and red jasper. While two yellowed ponies carve past

and we scatter all the ways there are to slip off rocks, plunge deep in corned snow.

Their cart, their woman, this late afternoon's burnished undulation, their supple leather lines.

As If the Sky Can Be Pressed

As if land can hold still. Look here. Where it bubbles up. Where the elk discriminate between fingertip leaves of sage and bitterbrush. And the soft petals of pink or white. A life cycle that crests in spikes that rip your eyes blind

where wings of wind turbines machete. Knife into the waves of navy blue. Silk rivulets. Pockmarked clouds.

Go ahead.

Try.

Hold the sky.

Press the land flat.

The deep fur of us. White dogs. Spice and cream goats. Sweep of their horns. Get out of my path you. I still fight just to walk forward. To keep on while you snake my ankles and tongue my fingers.

And the men that derail. Are they any different? The way they ice hard like a flat-rock hand-skipped? The curl of my mother's cigarette smoke as she watches on. Eggshell promises where I am the raw egg with a broken yoke slipping between ring and middle finger.

All of you crouch with me in this garden that is only allowed catastrophic weeding. All of you cling like sticky vines. All of you whimper in my ears even as I watch you nibble crisp crackers. With salt. Oh, this wind is howling. Until at last, I will find you all tooth-picked into the corners of barbed wire.

One more October

I will wrap my arms around. These decimated sticks and branches of you. By the bushel-full. These bare bones of you. This brushfire exploding into the next dry season.

Acknowledgments

With gratitude to the editors of the following publications in which these poems first appeared, sometimes in different versions:

Cirque: A Literary Journal for the North Pacific Rim (Vol. 13. No. 2): "As If the Sky Can Be Pressed," Pushcart Nomination, 2023.

The Shrub-Steppe Poetry Journal: (Spring, 2019): "Late Lunch Dakota Café" (Spring, 2019); "Upper Peoh Fire-Lookout" (Spring 2023); and "New Brand of Syncopation" (Spring 2024)

Quartet Journal (Spring 2024): "Like a Matriarchal Elephant" (as "Tractor designed with a cold-start")

Early Praise

In *Hags on Tractors,* Penny Johnson's poems enter the land and finger the coloring change of beige mushroom, vermillion tomatoes, evergreen rosemary, fat-thumbed blackberries, magenta holly hocks in her deeply porous study under the unforgiving sky. *And look, the blue-veined kale sprouting into its own life, cycles free-faced from dirt.* So it is: Johnson *sprouts into her own life,* wrangles more free, wrangles men and their useful love of tractors, shared or not, as earth-bound becomes earth-moving glory. The memory wounds of *father-mother curd* slip past an unhinged pasture gate, propped open or shut, and voices release, *Who do you think you are?* Safety is not lost or found but falls into the earth where Johnson stands her ground with pale wolf dogs and alabaster-hooved black mare close by. *Look,* she says again, at the wonder grown past haunting, *Tonight, I brew this soup of vermillion tomatoes plucked out of frost, whose cracks are barely sealed over with opaque filament. This glue.* The sealing of her heart without regret, she crescendos *the Howl/ in polished moon.* She ingests this place, *As if land can hold still* all it burns, buries and brings alive. Johnson's poems direct us: *Try./ Hold the sky.* And thereby announces our disappearing into the ground.

—Beatrix Gates, author of *The Burning Key: New & Selected Poems (1973-2023)*

The power of these poems is due to the simple fact that Johnson has invented a language using English words that resembles to great effect the nature of trauma, disassociation, sexuality, cars, boys, horses.

—Michael Kline, author of *When I Was a Twin*

It's difficult to say what is most intriguing about Penny Johnson's poems here. Maybe it's the fresh language that enthralls us with its sounds.

Maybe it's the vivid and startling images that leap off the page. Maybe it's the way Johnson thumbs her nose at tradition, engaging us through a structure which floats and spins and turns in on itself. Whatever it is, her poems bring the rural scene to life with all its sights, smells, sounds, tastes and challenges. Memory plays a role here, too, and Johnson leads us deftly back and forth between the now and the then. These are poems to be tasted, smelled and read over and over again.

—Susan Blair, author of *A Howling* **and** *What Remains of a Life,* **and editor of** *The Shrub-Steppe Poetry Journal*

About the Author

Penny Johnson lives at the base of a mountain with a horde of animals in Central Washington. She and her horse run the farm. Johnson provides glimpses of extraordinary lives that have lost some scaffolding but radiate genuine and quixotic vulnerability. Johnson's writing is visual and tactile. She has been featured poet in literary reviews and a contender in Seattle Poetry Slams. Johnson was the recipient of the Kirkwood Award for Short Fiction through UCLA Extension. She was a resident of Devereux, received her BA from The Evergreen State College, MFA from Goddard College. Both Johnson's novels, *Memories of a Female Truck Driver* and *Double Back*, are available from Amazon. She is a contributor in the *WA129* anthology with poems previously published in *Bellowing Ark, Pawn to Infinity, Spectacles, City Primevil,* and *Spillway.* Johnson has most recently been published in *Yakima Coffee House Poets* where she won the Tom Pier Prize, *Shrub-Steppe Review*, and *Cirque: A Literary Journal for the North Pacific Rim*, with a Pushcart Prize nomination, *Cleaver* (Fall 2023), Honorable Mention judged by Diane Suess and *Quartet Journal.*

About The Poetry Box®

The Poetry Box, a boutique publishing company in Portland, Oregon, provides a platform for both established and emerging poets to share their words with the world through beautiful printed books and chapbooks.

Feel free to visit the online bookstore (thePoetryBox.com), where you'll find more titles including:

metal used for beauty alone by Claudia F. Saleeby Savage

Lighting Up the Duff by Sheila Sondik

Now Is What Matters by Janet Steward

Blue Chip Stamp Guitar by Sue Fagalde Lick

The Hills Around Are Dust & Light by Karen Gookin

The Call Home by Susan Johnson

When All Else Fails by Lana Hechtman Ayers

Lamplight by Cathy Cain

Field Notes from an Illusion by Lois Levinson

White Sail at Midnight by Ginny Lowe Connors

What She Was Wearing by Shawn Aveningo Sanders

This Is the Lightness by Rachel Barton

Self Dissection by Amelia Diaz Ettinger

Remote Control by Laura Esther Sciortino

Transition Thunderstorms by Beth Bonness

and more . . .

www.ingramcontent.com/pod-product-compliance
Lightning Source LLC
LaVergne TN
LVHW050027080526
838202LV00069B/6958